HOW I FAILED TODAY

A daily journal encouraging
risk, resilience, and rebounding stronger.

Jennifer Jacob

Published by CreateSpace

FROM THE AUTHOR

It should be noted that I do not consider myself a subject matter expert on success, but rather an expert level achiever in failure. I don't consider myself to be bad at my job, lacking in income, or a disappointment to my family, but I prefer to think of myself as a risk-taker and challenge-facer. There are few things in this world that were successful upon first attempt, which means that to succeed, you must fail brilliantly (again and again). I wear my failures as a badge of honor, because it means that I am trying, and I would rather live a life knowing that I am giving it my "best go" versus playing it safe. This book was inspired by podcasts, seminars, and interviews with entrepreneurs that all share the same message: to fail is a crucial ingredient in the recipe of a successful and fulfilled life.

It is my hope that everyone that looks at this journal recognizes that failing is a single step on the way to something beautiful and that resilience is the true characteristic of those who go on to achieve their dreams. Because of this, I feel that admitting defeat or recognizing obstacles will allow everyone who takes this 100 day journey to celebrate all of the little moments that lead to the very big ones. We should all be *proud* to fail....and fail again...and again.

- Jennifer Stuart

INTRODUCTION

Every single person on the planet has one thing in common (okay, yes...we all breathe, eat, have organs, etc.), but we all, without a shadow of a doubt, *fail.*

Is that a negative perception? Not at all. In fact, you are about to see that some of the best minds in history, most successful entrepreneurs, and impactful philosophers believe that failure is one of the two pivotal factors in success (hint: you are one of them).

What is the second factor? Resilience. Resilience in the face of failure is arguably the most important ingredient to success.

As a fact, we will all fail. Everyone does it, but not everyone resilient. But then again, "everyone" isn't YOU.

Failure is to be celebrated, it is a badge of honor, and a stepping stone on the way to greatness. So let's pop the champagne and cue the fireworks, because you are about to record 100 days of failed attempts, mistakes, and obstacles that will lead you to becoming your best self.

Who is that? Well, I guess we are about to find out...aren't we?

GETTING STARTED

Before we get started on you 100 days of failure...

How do you define failure?

_____

_____

How do you feel about failure?

_____

_____

How do you define success?

_____

_____

What do you want to get out of this book?

_____

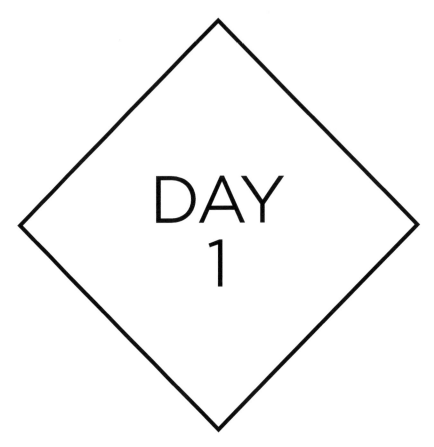

DAY
1

"Everything you want
is on the other side of fear."

- Jack Canfield

DAY 1

My biggest failure today was...

_____

_____

Through my failure, I learned...

_____

_____

_____

I plan to move forward through this failure by...

_____

_____

DAY
2

"Success is most often achieved by
those who don't know that
failure is inevitable."

- Coco Chanel

DAY 2

_____

My biggest failure today was...

_____

_____

Through my failure, I learned...

_____

_____

_____

My failure was inevitable because...

_____

_____

DAY
3

"Only those who dare to fail greatly
can ever achieve greatly."

- Robert F. Kennedy

DAY 3

My biggest failure today was...

_____

_____

Through my failure, I learned...

_____

_____

_____

The impacts of my failure were...

_____

_____

DAY 4

"What is the point of being alive if you don't at least try to do something remarkable?"

- John Green

DAY 4

My biggest failure today was...

My failure was impacted by...

Even though I failed, I am proud that I tried because...

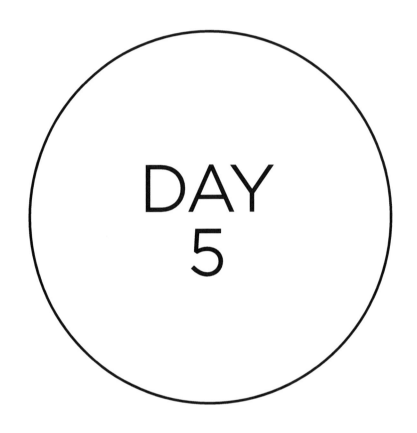

DAY
5

"With a hint of good judgment,
to fear nothing, not failure
or suffering or even death,
indicates that you value life the most.
You live to the extreme; you push
limits; you spend your time building
legacies. Those do not die."

- Criss Jami

DAY 5

My biggest failure today was...

_____

_____

Through my failure, I learned...

_____

_____

_____

My failure shaped my legacy by...

_____

_____

GO BIG

or

Go Home

Before we go further….

What do you consider your biggest failure of your life so far? And why?

_____

_____

How did it shape who you are?

_____

_____

What did you take away from your failure?

_____

_____

Have any successes come from what you learned?

_____

_____

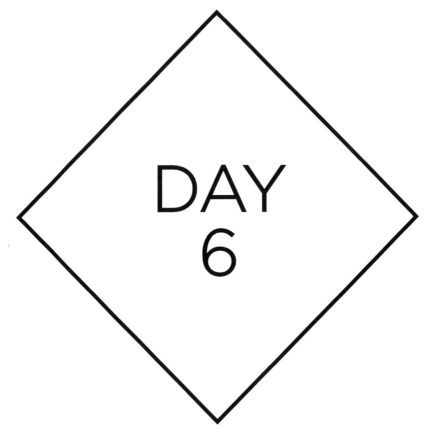

DAY
6

"It's not how far you fall,
but how high you bounce that counts."

- Zig Ziglar

DAY 6

My biggest failure today was...

_____

_____

Through my failure, I learned...

_____

_____

_____

I'll bounce back from my failure because...

_____

_____

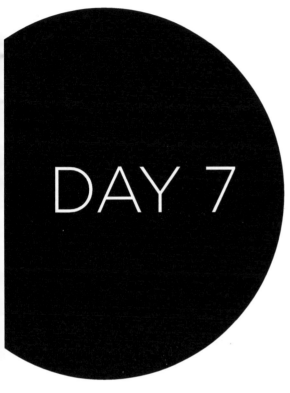

DAY 7

"Failure is so important.
We speak about success all the time.
It is the ability to resist failure or use
failure that often leads to greater
success. I've met people who don't
want to try for fear of failing."

- J.K. Rowling

DAY 7

My biggest failure today was...

_____

_____

Through my failure, I learned...

_____

_____

_____

When I talk about my failure, I will say that...

_____

_____

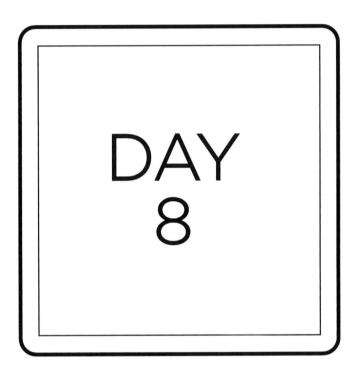

DAY
8

"You build on failure.
You use it as a stepping stone.
Close the door on the past.
You don't try to forget the mistakes,
but you don't dwell on it.
You don't let it have any of your
energy, or any of your time, or any of
your space."

- Johnny Cash

DAY 8

My biggest failure today was...

Through my failure, I learned...

This failure is a stepping stone to...

DAY 9

"We are all failures -
at least the best of us are."

- J.M. Barrie

DAY 9

My biggest failure today was...

_____

_____

Through my failure, I learned...

_____

_____

_____

I plan to move forward through this failure by...

_____

_____

DAY
10

"The only real mistake is the one from which we learn nothing."

- Henry Ford

DAY 10

My biggest failure today was...

_____

_____

Through my failure, I learned...

_____

_____

_____

I plan to move forward through this failure by...

_____

_____

"The greater the
obstacle,
the more glory in
overcoming it."

- Moliere

Let's think about this for a minute...

What has been the biggest challenge of your life?

_____

_____

How did you overcome it?

_____

_____

Did you have any hiccups along the way?

_____

_____

What value did those obstacles serve?

_____

_____

DAY
11

"Success is stumbling from failure to failure with no loss of enthusiasm."

- Winston Churchill

DAY 11

My biggest failure today was...

_____

_____

Through my failure, I learned...

_____

_____

_____

A success that I will have because of this failure is...

_____

_____

DAY 12

"Pain is temporary.
Quitting lasts forever."

- Lance Armstrong

DAY 12

My biggest failure today was...

Through my failure, I learned...

I will not quit because...

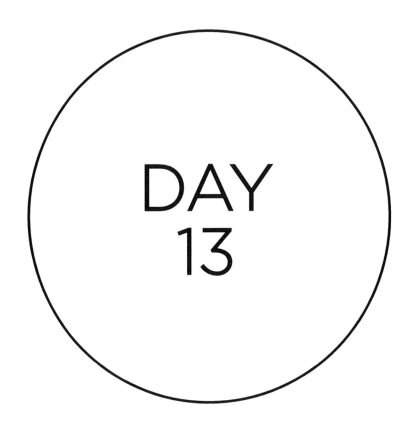

DAY
13

"There is only one thing that makes a
dream impossible to achieve:
the fear of failure."

- Paulo Coelho

DAY 13

My biggest failure today was...

_____

_____

Through my failure, I learned...

_____

_____

_____

I plan to move forward through this failure by...

_____

_____

DAY
14

"The test of strength is not avoiding
emotional distress;
it's functioning in the face of it."

- Megyn Kelly

DAY 14

My biggest failure today was...

_____

_____

Through my failure, I learned...

_____

_____

_____

I couldn't be successful without this failure because...

_____

_____

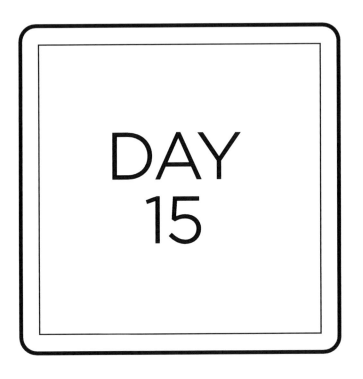

DAY
15

"No human ever became interesting by not failing. The more you fail and recover and improve, the better you are as a person. Ever meet someone who's always had everything work out for them with zero struggle? They usuallyhave the depth of a puddle. Or they don't exist."

- Chris Hardwick

DAY 15

My biggest failure today was...

_____

_____

Through my failure, I learned...

_____

_____

_____

I plan to move forward through this failure by...

_____

_____

Let's try something…
and be really honest
with yourself.

We are going to go
"7 Levels Deep"
on what drives you towards
your vision of success.

What is your goal in life (you can be as general or as specific as you want).

_____

_____

Why do you have that goal?

_____

_____

Ask yourself "why" again, about your previous answer.

_____

_____

Keep going....ask yourself "why" about the last answer.

_____

_____

*Question inspired by and credited to Real Estate expert, Dean Graziozi

You get the pattern...

_____

_____

Yes...again.

_____

_____

Almost there.

_____

_____

One more time.

_____

_____

DAY 16

"Only those who dare to fail greatly
can ever achieve greatly."

- Robert F. Kennedy

DAY 16

My biggest failure today was...

_____

_____

Through my failure, I learned...

_____

_____

_____

I plan to move forward through this failure by...

_____

_____

DAY
17

"Failure should be our teacher,
not our undertaker. Failure is delay,
not defeat. It is a temporary detour,
not a dead end. Failure is something
we can avoid only by saying nothing,
doing nothing, and being nothing."

- Denis Waitley

DAY 17

My biggest failure today was...

Through my failure, I learned...

I will be responsible for my failure because it makes me better at...

DAY 18

"When you take risks, you learn that there will be times when you succeed and there will be times when you fail, and both are equally important."

- Ellen DeGeneres

DAY 18

My biggest failure today was...

Through my failure, I learned...

I took a risk today by...

DAY
19

"I have not failed.
I've just found 10,000 ways
that won't work."

- Thomas A. Edison

DAY 19

My biggest failure today was...

_____

_____

Through my failure, I learned...

_____

_____

_____

I plan to move forward through this failure by...

_____

_____

DAY 20

"Every adversity, every failure, every heartache carries with it the seed of an equal or greater benefit."

- Napoleon Hill

DAY 20

My biggest failure today was...

Through my failure, I learned...

This failure will benefit me by...

TIME OUT...

"We rise by lifting others" Robert Ingersoll

Who has had the biggest impact on your life?

_____

Why?

_____

_____

What is the most important lesson they taught you?

_____

_____

Do you know about any adversities they faced?

_____

_____

How has their resilience impacted you?

_____

_____

DAY
21

"Winners are not afraid of losing.
But losers are. Failure is part of the
process of success. People who avoid
failure also avoid success."

- Robert T. Kiyosaki

DAY 21

My biggest failure today was...

If I hadn't failed, I would have learned...

My failure was important because...

DAY
22

"Success is not final, failure is not fatal:
it is the courage to continue
that counts."

- Winston Churchill

DAY 22

My biggest failure today was...

_____

_____

Through my failure, I learned...

_____

_____

_____

My failure is not final because I will have the courage to...

_____

_____

DAY 23

"It's failure that gives you the proper perspective on success."

- Ellen DeGeneres

DAY 23

_____

My biggest failure today was...

_____

_____

Through my failure, I learned...

_____

_____

_____

Success will taste a little sweeter because...

_____

_____

DAY
24

"Failure should be our teacher, not our undertaker. Failure is delay, not defeat. It is a temporary detour, not a dead end. Failure is something we can avoid onlyby saying nothing, doing nothing, and being nothing."

- Denis Waitley

DAY 24

My biggest failure today was...

_____

_____

Through my failure, I learned...

_____

_____

_____

Failing was better than lack of action because...

_____

_____

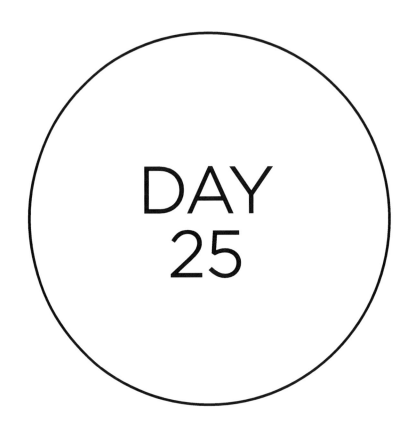

DAY
25

"If you don't try at anything,
you can't fail...
It takes back bone to lead
the life you want."

- Richard Yates

DAY 25

My biggest failure today was...

_____

_____

Through my failure, I learned...

_____

_____

_____

I applaud myself for...

_____

_____

"Only in the darkness, can you see the stars."

- Martin Luther King, Jr.

Everyone has had a "dark day" where they've felt like the world was against them and nothing was going right.

What was your dark day? Get it all out...

_____

_____

How did you get through it?

_____

_____

What did you learn about yourself?

_____

_____

What is the best thing that came from that situation?

_____

_____

DAY 26

"Giving up is the only sure way to fail."

- Gena Showalter

DAY 26

My biggest failure today was...

_____

_____

Through my failure, I learned...

_____

_____

_____

I refuse to let my failure impact my goals because...

_____

_____

DAY
27

"If you're not prepared to be wrong,
you'll never come up with
anything original."

- Ken Robinson

DAY 27

My biggest failure today was...

_____

_____

Through my failure, I learned...

_____

_____

_____

I'm comfortable with my failure today because...

_____

_____

DAY 28

"The phoenix must burn to emerge."

- Janet Fitch

DAY 28

My biggest failure today was...

_____

_____

Through my failure, I learned...

_____

_____

_____

I plan to move forward through this failure by...

_____

_____

DAY
29

"Do not be embarrassed by your
failures, learn from them
and start again."

- Richard Branson

DAY 29

My biggest failure today was...

_____

_____

Through my failure, I learned...

_____

_____

_____

I won't be embarrassed by my failure because...

_____

_____

DAY
30

"Victory is sweetest when you've known defeat."

- Malcolm S. Forbes

DAY 30

My biggest failure today was...

_____

_____

Through my failure, I learned...

_____

_____

_____

One thing that I did great today was...

_____

_____

"Comparison
is the thief of joy."

- Theodore Roosevelt

Not to bring it up, but....

Who has made you feel poorly about yourself?

_____

_____

How has this impacted your self-image?

_____

_____

How has this impacted how you see others?

_____

_____

How has this impacted how you treat others?

_____

_____

Funny how that works, huh?

DAY 31

"I cannot give you the formula for success, but I can give you the formula for failure which is:
Try to please everybody."

- Herbert B. Swope

DAY 31

My biggest failure today was...

Through my failure, I learned...

I plan to move forward through this failure by...

DAY
32

"Love yourself first and everything else falls into line. You really have to love yourself to get anything done in this world."

- Lucille Ball

DAY 32

My biggest failure today was...

Through my failure, I learned...

I will love myself, with all my faults, because...

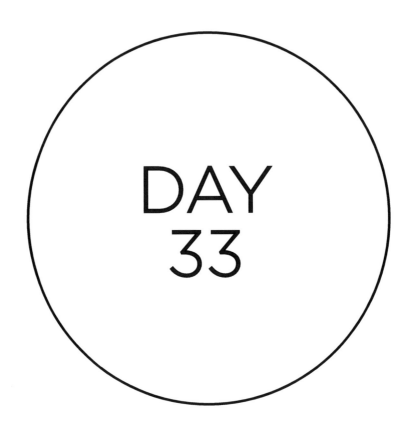

DAY
33

"Success is not measured by what you accomplish, but by the opposition you have encountered, and the courage with which you have maintained the struggle against overwhelming odds."

- Orison Swett Marden

DAY 33

My biggest failure today was...

_____

_____

Through my failure, I learned...

_____

_____

_____

I will beat the odds of not repeating my failure by...

_____

_____

DAY
34

"Success does not consist in never making mistakes but in never making the same one a second time."

- George Shaw

DAY 34

My biggest failure today was...

_____

_____

Through my failure, I learned...

_____

_____

_____

I won't make this mistake again because...

_____

_____

DAY
35

"I attribute my success to this:
I never gave or took any excuse."

- Florence Nightingale

DAY 35

My biggest failure today was...

_____

_____

Through my failure, I learned...

_____

_____

_____

I choose to be accountable for my failure, but I could have made the excuse that...

_____

_____

_____

If it were your last day on earth and you could leave the world with **3** things that you know to be true, what would they be?

1.

_____

_____

2.

_____

_____

3.

_____

_____

*Question inspired by the Podcast "The School of Greatness" by Lewis Howes

DAY 36

"Spend eighty percent of your time focusing on the opportunities of tomorrow rather than the problems of yesterday."

- Brian Tracey

DAY 36

My biggest failure today was...

_____

_____

Through my failure, I learned...

_____

_____

_____

Because of my failure, I have the opportunity to...

_____

_____

DAY
37

"If the only tool you have is a hammer, you tend to see every problem as a nail."

- Abraham Maslow

DAY 37

My biggest failure today was...

Through my failure, I learned...

My failure is not a failure at all because...

DAY 38

"Whenever you're in conflict
with someone, there is one factor
that can make the difference between
damaging your relationship and
deepening it. That factor is attitude."

- William James

DAY 38

My biggest failure today was...

_____

_____

Through my failure, I learned...

_____

_____

_____

Moving forward, my relationships will become deeper because...

_____

_____

DAY
39

"There are two types of people
who will tell you that you cannot make
a difference in this world:
those who are afraid to try and
those who are afraid you will succeed."

- Ray Goforth

DAY 39

My biggest failure today was...

_____

_____

Through my failure, I learned...

_____

_____

_____

My biggest fear is...

_____

_____

DAY 40

"After every difficulty, ask yourself two
questions: "What did I do right?" and
"What would I do differently?"

- Brian Tracey

DAY 40

My biggest failure today was...

_____

_____

Through my failure, I learned...

_____

_____

_____

What I did right today was...

_____

_____

The difference
between who you are
and who you want to be, is

what you do.

Write 5 characteristics of the person that you want to become.

1.
_____

2.
_____

3.
_____

4.
_____

5.
_____

Who is someone that you consider to have these qualities?

_____

What can you do on a daily basis to be the person with your 5 ideal characteristics?

_____

_____

DAY
41

"Life's real failure is when you do not realize how close you were to success when you gave up."

- Unknown

DAY 41

My biggest failure today was...

Through my failure, I learned...

I plan to move forward through this failure by...

DAY
42

"If you're going through hell,
keep going."

- Winston Churchill

DAY 42

My biggest failure today was...

_____

_____

Despite my failure, I am closer to success because...

_____

_____

_____

I plan to move forward through this failure by...

_____

_____

DAY
43

"Be miserable. Or motivate yourself.
Whatever has to be done, it's always
your choice."

- Wayne Dyer

DAY 43

My biggest failure today was...

Through my failure, I learned...

Because of what I learned today, tomorrow I choose to...

DAY 44

"Judge your success by what you had to give up in order to get it."

- Dalai Lama

DAY 44

My biggest failure today was...

_____

_____

Through my failure, I learned...

_____

_____

_____

I plan to move forward through this failure by...

_____

_____

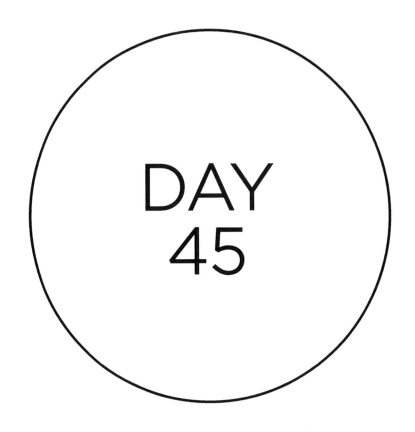

DAY
45

"People who succeed have momentum. The more they succeed, the more they want to succeed, and the more they find a way to succeed. Similarly, when someone is failing, the tendency is to get on a downward spiral that can even become a self-fulfilling prophecy."

- Tony Robbins

DAY 45

My biggest failure today was...

_____

_____

Through my failure, I learned...

_____

_____

_____

This failure will not disrupt my momentum because...

_____

_____

Work
until your idols become your equals.

Who is your business idol?

_____

_____

What is admirable about them?

_____

_____

How did they reach their achievements?

_____

_____

What is one thing that you can do each day that have helped them become successful?

_____

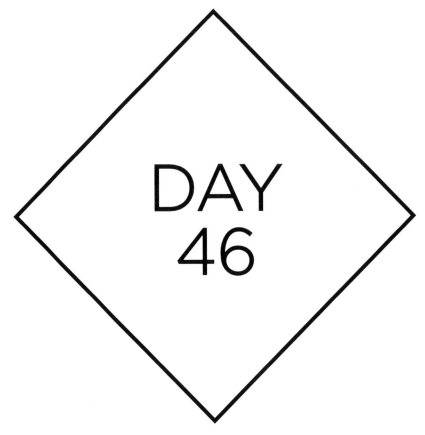

DAY
46

"Aim for success, not perfection.
Never give up your right to be wrong,
because then you will lose the ability
to learn new things and move forward
with your life. Remember that fear
always lurks behind perfectionism."

- David Burns

DAY 46

My biggest failure today was...

_____

_____

Through my failure, I learned...

_____

_____

_____

I am not perfect, but I am...

_____

_____

DAY 47

"Success seems to be connected
with action. Successful people keep
moving. They make mistakes,
but they don't quit."

- Conrad Hilton

DAY 47

My biggest failure today was...

Through my failure, I learned...

I will not quit because...

DAY
48

"The difference between a successful person and others is not a lack of strength, not a lack of knowledge, but rather a lack of will."

- Vince Lombardi

DAY 48

My biggest failure today was...

_____

_____

Through my failure, I learned...

_____

_____

_____

I plan to move forward through this failure by...

_____

_____

DAY 49

"Keep away from people who try to belittle your ambitions. Small people always do that, but the really great make you feel that you, too, can become great."

- Mark Twain

DAY 49

My biggest failure today was...

Through my failure, I learned...

I was empowered today by...

DAY
50

"Success is how high you bounce
when you hit bottom."

- George Patton

DAY 50

_____

My biggest failure today was...

_____

_____

Through my failure, I learned...

_____

_____

_____

I plan to move forward through this failure by...

_____

_____

You're

HALFWAY

there!

What has been your biggest failure in the past 50 days?

_____

_____

Did you view it differently than failures in the past?

_____

_____

How so?

_____

_____

What is the biggest lesson that you've learned in the past 50 days?

_____

_____

DAY
51

"Ever tried. Ever failed. No matter.
Try Again. Fail again. Fail better."

- Samuel Beckett

DAY 51

My biggest failure today was...

_____

_____

Through my failure, I learned...

_____

_____

_____

I will try again because...

_____

_____

DAY 52

"What seems to us as bitter trials are often blessings in disguise."

- Oscar Wilde

DAY 52

My biggest failure today was...

_____

_____

Through my failure, I learned...

_____

_____

_____

I plan to move forward through this failure by...

_____

_____

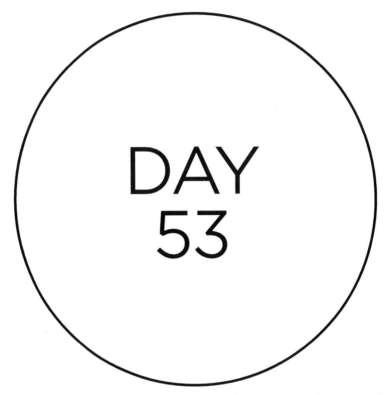

DAY
53

"Don't wait until everything is just right.
It will never be perfect. There will always
be challenges, obstacles and less than
perfect conditions. So what. Get started
now. With each step you take, you
will grow stronger and stronger,
more and more skilled,
more and more self-confident
and more and more successful."

- Mark Victor Hansen

DAY 53

My biggest failure today was...

Through my failure, I learned...

The step that I will take today to become my best self is...

DAY
54

"The successful warrior is the average man, with laser-like focus."

- Bruce Lee

DAY 54

My biggest failure today was...

Through my failure, I learned...

I plan to move forward through this failure by...

DAY
55

"Live as if you were to die tomorrow.
Learn as if you were to live forever."

- Mahatma Ghandi

DAY 55

My biggest failure today was...

_____

_____

Through my failure, I learned...

_____

_____

_____

If today were my last day, I hope that my legacy would be...

_____

_____

"It's risky. It's scary.
It's terrifying to jump.
There's a huge chance it
won't work out.
That's the point.
Be brave.
Do it anyway."

- The Better Man Project

What is the bravest thing that you have ever done?

_____

_____

Did you face any obstacles?

_____

_____

If no... WOW! Congratulations!

If yes, how did your resilience impact the outcome?

_____

_____

DAY 56

"The road to success is always under construction."

\- Lily Tomlin

DAY 56

My biggest failure today was...

Through my failure, I learned...

The thing that I am most proud of today is...

DAY
57

"If people did not do silly things,
nothing intelligent would ever get done."

- Ludwig Wittgenstein

DAY 57

My biggest failure today was...

_____

_____

Through my failure, I learned...

_____

_____

_____

The silliest thing that I did today was...

_____

_____

DAY 58

"I find that the harder I work,
the more luck I seem to have."

- Thomas Jefferson

DAY 58

My biggest failure today was...

_____

_____

Through my failure, I learned...

_____

_____

_____

I'm grateful for my opportunity to fail because...

_____

_____

DAY
59

"Don't let the fear of losing be greater than the excitement of winning."

- Robert Kiyosaki

DAY 59

My biggest failure today was...

_____

_____

Through my failure, I learned...

_____

_____

_____

I plan to move forward through this failure by...

_____

_____

DAY 60

"Whenever you see a successful person, you only see the public glories, never the private sacrifices to reach them."

- Vaibhav Shah

DAY 60

My biggest failure today was...

_____

_____

Through my failure, I learned...

_____

_____

_____

One sacrifice I made to get closer to my goals was...

_____

_____

So, on a **personal** note...

When's a time that you hurt someone's feelings?

_____

_____

How did you fail to consider their feelings?

_____

_____

What was the resolution (if any)?

_____

_____

How is that relationship now?

_____

We can only control our own reactions, so what could you have done differently in the situation?

_____

DAY
61

"I've missed more than 9000 shots in my career. I've lost almost 300 games. 26 times, I've been trusted to take the game winning shot and missed. I've failed over and over and over again in my life. And that is why I succeed."

- Michael Jordan

DAY 61

My biggest failure today was...

_____

_____

Through my failure, I learned...

_____

_____

_____

I will enthusiastically continue to fail because...

_____

_____

DAY
62

"Success comes in cans;
failure in can'ts."

- Unknown

DAY 62

My biggest failure today was...

_____

_____

Through my failure, I learned...

_____

_____

_____

I plan to move forward through this failure by...

_____

_____

DAY 63

"Patience, persistence and perspiration
make an unbeatable combination
for success."

- Napolean Hill

DAY 63

My biggest failure today was...

_____

_____

Through my failure, I learned...

_____

_____

_____

I exercised patience with myself today by...

_____

_____

DAY
64

"Life will bring you pain all by itself.
Your responsibility is to create joy."

- Milton Erickson

DAY 64

My biggest failure today was...

_____

_____

Through my failure, I learned...

_____

_____

_____

I choose joy in spite of failure because...

_____

_____

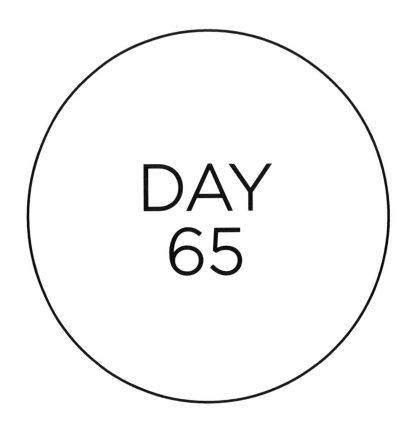

DAY
65

"If you are not willing to risk the usual,
you will have to settle for the ordinary."

- Jim Rohn

DAY 65

My biggest failure today was...

_____

_____

Through my failure, I learned...

_____

_____

_____

I won't settle for ordinary because...

_____

_____

I'm going to make you so proud!

- Note to self

What are you most proud of?

_____

_____

What did you have to give up to get it/do it?

_____

_____

Did it make it make your achievement more valuable?

_____

If yes, how so?

_____

_____

Did anyone help you along the way? _____

If yes, this is your gentle reminder to thank them...wink, wink

DAY 66

"You don't have to see the whole staircase, just take the first step."

- Martin Luther King, Jr.

DAY 66

My biggest failure today was...

_____

_____

Through my failure, I learned...

_____

_____

_____

I plan to move forward through this failure by...

_____

_____

DAY
67

"Our greatest fear should not be
of failure...but of succeeding at things
in life that don't really matter."

- Francis Chan

DAY 67

My biggest failure today was...

_____

_____

Through my failure, I learned...

_____

_____

_____

My failure matters because...

_____

_____

DAY 68

"The thing that is really hard, and really amazing, is giving up on being perfect and beginning the work of becoming yourself."

- Anna Quindlen

DAY 68

My biggest failure today was...

This failure helped me get closer to my best self because...

I plan to move forward through this failure by...

DAY
69

"Good judgment comes from experience.
Experience comes from bad judgment."

- Jim Horning

DAY 69

My biggest failure today was...

_____

_____

Through my failure, I learned...

_____

_____

_____

I will show good judgement in future by...

_____

_____

DAY
70

"The truth will set you free,
but first it will piss you off."

- Gloria Steinem

DAY 70

My biggest failure today was...

Through my failure, I learned...

I plan to move forward through this failure by...

We often **learn** from **watching** others...

What is a mistake than someone else has made that gave you perspective to avoid doing the same?

_____

_____

Did it change their behavior moving forward?

_____

What potential mistakes have you avoided by learning from seeing their failure?

_____

_____

How has this been valuable?

_____

_____

DAY 71

"However long the night,
the dawn will break."

- African Proverb

DAY 71

My biggest failure today was...

_____

_____

Through my failure, I learned...

_____

_____

_____

I know that I can overcome this failure by...

_____

_____

DAY
72

"The cave you fear to enter
holds the treasure you seek."

- Joseph Campbell

DAY 72

My biggest failure today was...

_____

_____

Because of my failure today, I fear...

_____

_____

_____

I plan to move forward through this failure by...

_____

_____

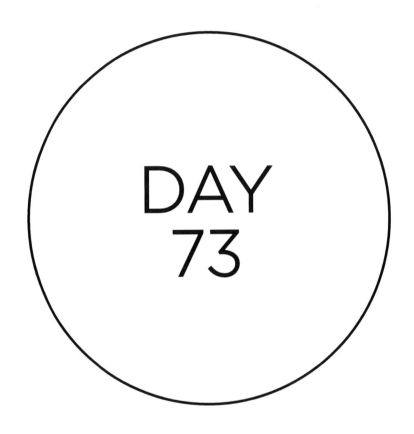

DAY
73

"90% of life is about remaining calm."

- Dr. Chris Feudtner

DAY 73

My biggest failure today was...

_____

_____

Through my failure, I learned...

_____

_____

_____

I plan to move forward through this failure by...

_____

_____

DAY
74

"The difference between a strong man and a weak one is that the former does not give up after a defeat."

- Woodrow Wilson

DAY 74

My biggest failure today was...

_____

_____

After I failed, I felt...

_____

_____

_____

Because of how I felt, I plan to...

_____

_____

DAY
75

"It may sound strange, but many champions are made champions by setbacks."

- Bob Richards

DAY 75

My biggest failure today was...

_____

_____

Through my failure, I learned...

_____

_____

_____

I plan to move forward through this failure by...

_____

_____

"Yesterday I was clever, so I wanted to change the world. Today, I am wise, so I am changing myself."

- Unknown

How have you adapted your personal or professional approach to become more successful in reaching a goal?

_____

_____

Why do feel like adapting was important for your particular scenario?

_____

_____

What could have happened if you didn't adapt?

_____

_____

DAY 76

"Our greatest glory is not in never falling, but in rising every time we fall."

\- Confucius

DAY 76

My biggest failure today was...

_____

_____

Through my failure, I learned...

_____

_____

_____

I plan to move forward through this failure by...

_____

_____

DAY
77

"The farther backward you can look,
the farther forward you are likely to see."

- Winston Churchill

DAY 77

My biggest failure today was...

_____

_____

Looking back, I feel that I will appreciate this failure because...

_____

_____

_____

I plan to move forward through this failure by...

_____

_____

DAY 78

"The bamboo that bends is stronger
than the oak that resists."

- Japanese Proverb

DAY 78

My biggest failure today was...

I accept responsibility for this failure because...

I plan to move forward through this failure by...

DAY
79

"The world breaks everyone,
and afterward, some are strong at
the broken places."

- Ernest Hemingway

DAY 79

My biggest failure today was...

_____

_____

Through my failure, I learned...

_____

_____

_____

I will be stronger tomorrow because...

_____

_____

DAY 80

"Things don't go wrong and break your heart so you can become bitter and give up. They happen to break you down and build you up so you can be all you were intended to be."

- Charles Jones

DAY 80

My biggest failure today was...

_____

_____

This failure provided me with the perspective that...

_____

_____

_____

I plan to move forward through this failure by...

_____

_____

Now that you know more about yourself than you did yesterday,

let's dig **deeper...**

If you could give advice to the 10 year old version of yourself, what would you say?

_____

_____

10 years from now, what do you think you will regret *not* doing?

_____

_____

So, what is holding you back from *actually* doing it? Fear? Money? Relationships?

_____

_____

Have you ever thought that the only thing holding you back, is the thought that something is holding you back? ...Yeah...let that marinate.

DAY
81

"Forget mistakes. Forget failures.
Forget everything except what you
are going to do right now, and do it.
Today is your lucky day."

- Will Durant

DAY 81

My biggest failure today was...

_____

_____

Through my failure, I learned...

_____

_____

_____

Today has shaped who I am by...

_____

_____

DAY
82

"Someone was hurt before you, wronged before you, hungry before you, frightened before you, beaten before you, humiliated before you, raped before you? Yet, someone survived? You can do anything you choose to do."

- Maya Angelou

DAY 82

My biggest failure today was...

_____

_____

Through my failure, I learned...

_____

_____

_____

I choose to celebrate this failure by...

_____

_____

DAY 83

"Fall seven times, stand up eight."

- Japanese Proverb

DAY 83

My biggest failure today was...

_____

_____

Through my failure, I learned...

_____

_____

_____

I plan to move forward through this failure by...

_____

_____

DAY
84

"Although the world is full of suffering,
it is also full of the overcoming of it."

- Helen Keller

DAY 84

My biggest failure today was...

_____

_____

Through my failure, I learned...

_____

_____

_____

I plan to overcome this obstacle by...

_____

_____

DAY
85

"When we learn how to become resilient, we learn how to embrace the beautifully broad spectrum of the human experience."

- Jaeda Dewalt

DAY 85

My biggest failure today was...

Through my failure, I learned...

Through this failure, I experienced...

"The cost of being wrong, is less than the cost of doing nothing."

- Seth Godin

Write down a little bit about a time where you really hated to be wrong...but you were.

How did you react?

Are you proud of how you reacted?

In retrospect, would you have changed how you reacted?

DAY 86

"Resilience is very different than being numb. Resilience means you experience, you feel, you fail, you hurt. You fall. But, you keep going."

- Yasmin Mogahead

DAY 86

My biggest failure today was...

_____

_____

Through my failure, I learned...

_____

_____

_____

I plan to move forward through this failure by...

_____

_____

DAY
87

"We are not a product of what has
happened to us in our past.
We have the power of choice."

- Stephen Covey

DAY 87

My biggest failure today was...

_____

_____

Through my failure, I learned...

_____

_____

_____

I will choose to move past this by...

_____

_____

DAY 88

"Success is the result of perfection, hard work, learning from failure, loyalty, and persistence."

- Colin Powell

DAY 88

_____

My biggest failure today was...

_____

_____

Through my failure, I learned...

_____

_____

_____

I plan to move forward through this failure by...

_____

_____

DAY
89

"Success is a lousy teacher.
It seduces smart people into thinking
they can't lose."

- Bill Gates

DAY 89

My biggest failure today was...

_____

_____

Through my failure, I learned...

_____

_____

_____

This failure won't deter me from my goals because...

_____

_____

DAY
90

"Resilience is not what happens to you. It's how you react to, respond to, and recover from what happens to you."

- Jeffrey Gitomer

DAY 90

My biggest failure today was...

_____

_____

Through my failure, I learned...

_____

_____

_____

I will recover from this failure by...

_____

_____

So we think you are really great!

How do you define "greatness"?

_____

_____

How does this differ from your definition of "success"?

_____

_____

How do they overlap for you?

_____

_____

What can you do to become your perception of both "great" and "successful"?

_____

_____

*Question inspired by the Podcast "The School of Greatness" by Lewis Howes

DAY 91

"I wouldn't be where I am now
if I didn't fail...a lot.
The good, the bad, it's all part of the
success equation."

- Mark Cuban

DAY 91

My biggest failure today was...

_____

_____

Through my failure, I learned...

_____

_____

_____

The silver lining to this failure was...

_____

_____

DAY
92

"If you think you can do a thing or think you can't do a thing, you're right."

- Henry Ford

DAY 92

My biggest failure today was...

Through my failure, I learned...

Because of my failure, I was able to...

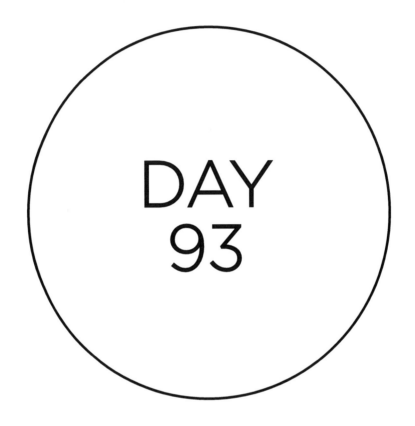

DAY
93

"The most dangerous poison is the feeling of achievement. The antidote is to, every evening, think what can be done better tomorrow."

- Ingvar Kamprad

DAY 93

My biggest failure today was...

_____

_____

Through my failure, I learned...

_____

_____

_____

I plan to move forward through this failure by...

_____

_____

DAY
94

"Develop success from failures.
Discouragement and failure are two
of the surest steppingstones to
success."

- Dale Carnegie

DAY 94

My biggest failure today was...

_____

_____

Through my failure, I learned...

_____

_____

_____

I plan to move forward through this failure by...

_____

_____

DAY
95

"I knew that if I failed I wouldn't regret that, but I knew the one thing I might regret is not trying."

- Jeff Bezos

DAY 95

My biggest failure today was...

_____

_____

Through my failure, I learned...

_____

_____

_____

I plan to move forward through this failure by...

_____

_____

We've all had times where our own **pride** has become our **biggest** obstacle.

What moment did your pride get in your own way?

_____

_____

How did this affect your relationships?

_____

_____

How did this impact your mood?

_____

_____

What positive came from you being prideful?

_____

_____

DAY 96

"I was set free, because my greatest fear had already been realized, and I was still alive, and I still had a daughter whom I adored, and I had an old typewriter and a big idea. And so rock bottom became the solid foundation on which I rebuilt my life."

- J.K. Rowling

DAY 96

My biggest failure today was...

Through my failure, I learned...

I plan to move forward through this failure by...

DAY
97

"I'm only rich because I know when I'm wrong...I basically have survived by recognizing my mistakes."

- George Soros

DAY 97

My biggest failure today was...

_____

_____

Through my failure, I learned...

_____

_____

_____

I plan to move forward through this failure by...

_____

_____

DAY 98

"Everyone experiences tough times;
it is a measure of your determination
and dedication how you deal
with them and how you can come
through them."

- Lakshmi Mittal

DAY 98

My biggest failure today was...

Through my failure, I learned...

I plan to move forward through this failure by...

DAY 99

"Failure is not the outcome -
failure is not trying.
Don't be afraid to fail."

- Sara Blakely

DAY 99

My biggest failure today was...

_____

_____

I felt...

_____

_____

_____

I plan to move forward through this failure by...

_____

_____

DAY 100

"It's fine to celebrate success but it is more important to heed the lessons of failure."

- Bill Gates

DAY 100

My biggest failure today was...

_____

_____

Through my failure, I learned...

_____

_____

_____

I will celebrate this lesson by...

_____

_____

You did it... You failed 100 times! That means 100 days of lessons, 100 decisions to show resilience, and 100 paces closer to a more successful YOU!

You're not done yet....let's bring it full circle!

Now, how do you define failure?

_____

_____

Do you feel the same about failure as when you started?

_____

_____

How do you define resilience?

_____

_____

What did you get out of this book?

YOU DID IT!

You failed...you owned it...and you kept going! And isn't that the whole point? You. Kept. Going. You did what many couldn't. You proved that obstacles won't hold you back from claiming what you know is yours. You took 100 days and turned them into the foundation of building your legacy.

I once heard someone say, "if you aren't embarrassed by your first version, then you aren't doing it right." Who cares if it was humbling, if you blushed a little, and if you made a fool of yourself (okay, well...hopefully not a *complete* fool), but you learned from your mistakes.

By now, I hope you know that failing isn't a negative thing. Failure is merely a temporary setback on the road to where you want to be. If you take a wrong turn, re-route and find a better map!

So, do you know what to do now? If you thought..."umm...fail some more?," you guessed right! That's the only thing to do to keep moving forward.

After all, the only way to guarantee failure is to stop trying. So keep going, keep trying, keep failing, keep learning, keep celebrating your successes (no matter how big or small), and don't stop....

EVER.

JENNIFER STUART started her career in Organizational Development, where she focused her efforts on encouraging the growth of her team members to accomplish more for the betterment of themselves and the organization. With a little gumption and a lot of hard work, she quit her corporate career to follow her passion of travel.

She is the CEO and proud founder of Explorateur Travel, LLC which creates custom itineraries with a focus on local culture. She plans to practice what she preaches and to fail everyday with reckless abandon.

Made in the USA
Columbia, SC
09 July 2017